THE
REDOUTÉ
ALBUM

THE REDOUTÉ ALBUM

INCLUDES A SUITE OF

Eighty-four Bouquets

NEVER BEFORE
PUBLISHED
AND A SELECTION FROM

The Lilies

PREFACE BY GRAHAM ARADER

THE OVERLOOK PRESS

WOODSTOCK, NEW YORK

Published in 1991 by
The Overlook Press
Lewis Hollow Road
Woodstock, New York 12498

The publisher wishes to thank the Graham Arader Galleries
for permission to reproduce works from their collection.

Photography by Sepp Seitz
Designed by Hannah Lerner

Library of Congress Cataloging-in-Publication Data

Redouté, Pierre-Joseph. 1759-1840.
    The Redouté album / introduction, Graham Arader.
      p.   cm.
    ISBN 0-87951-439-6
    1. Redouté, Pierre-Joseph. 1759-1840.   2. Botanical illustration—
France. 3. Flowers—Pictorial works. 4. Flower painting and
illustration—France. I. Title.
QK98.183.R43A2 1991   91-16726
581'.022—dc20   CIP

ISBN 0-87951-439-6

Printed in Italy

Preface

The most famous botanical artist who ever lived, and for many connoisseurs of plant illustration the finest of all flower painters, remains after nearly 200 years Pierre-Joseph Redouté. Although he has frequently been referred to as the "Raphael of flowers," a more apt comparison might be to his contemporary John James Audubon. Redouté, like the great American illustrator of birds and mammals, while undeniably a brilliant artist, is remembered as something more than solely an artistic phenomenon. Redouté's career, like Audubon's, also reflected the scientific spirit of the times.

Both artists were products of the Enlightenment, observing and recording nature's wonders from the dual perspective of a skilled artist-naturalist, and both men are now legendary figures from the age of Romanticism. They explored new fields of inquiry and disseminated information gathered by the elite for the benefit of a wider public by means of the print medium.

The story of Redouté's life reads like the plot of a popular historical novel. He was born in 1759 at Saint Hubert in the Belgian Ardennes and was descended from a line of journeyman painters. Redouté's father, Charles-Joseph Redouté, was also a painter, as had been his grandfather and great-grandfather before that. All three sons of the elder Redouté and his wife, Marie-Joseph, became apprenticed in the craft of painting to their father at a very early age.

When he was only thirteen years old, Pierre-Joseph felt himself sufficiently prepared to set off on his own to become a painter. He thus began a decade of wandering about which little is known. We can surmise, however, that he pursued an itinerant career as an artisan-decorator as his father and an older brother had done before him. We know only that he painted the walls of châteaus as readily as he executed commissioned portraits and probably other subjects as well.

When he was twenty-three, in 1782, Redouté made his way to Paris where he joined his elder brother, Antoine-Ferdinand, who worked as a painter of stage scenery for the Théâtre Italien. The younger artist now turned his hand to yet another painter's trade, but he was not destined to spend very many years painting stage sets. In his spare time he visited the Jardin du Roi where he studied and sketched the flowers and plants. For a young artist from the provinces there were certainly many artistic and cultural attractions to be discovered in the French capital. One can only imagine how stimulating it would have been to be in Paris on the very eve of the Revolution.

Gradually, Redouté found his true calling. According to statements he made in later years, because of his background he had long been familiar with the great Netherlands tradition of flower painting. He particularly admired the Dutch and

Flemish still life painters of the 17th century, including Jan van Huysums and the woman who arranged magical bouquets on canvas, Rachel Ruysh.

Some of the drawings he made during this period were published as engravings and attracted the attention of a wealthy amateur botanist named Charles Louis L'Hértier de Brutelle, who had undertaken to produce a series of books devoted to the current interest in plant cultivation. At this time many exotic plants were being introduced into Europe from colonial outposts around the globe. Redouté just happened to be the right artist in the right place at exactly the right moment in time.

L'Hértier saw in Redouté the potential he was seeking and set out to become his patron and teacher. Redouté already had acquired the artistry necessary for pleasing work, but L'Hértier instructed him in the science of plant anatomy and the techniques of dissection. After familiarizing himself with the contents of L'Hértier's private library and herbarium, Redouté soon learned to make drawings that were sufficiently detailed and scientifically accurate.

Redouté contributed 54 out of the 91 plates that appeared in *Stripes Novae*, a collection of "new herbs" published in parts by L'Hértier between 1784 and 1789. He seems, in fact, to have been aided by his younger brother Henri-Joseph and to have eventually taken over production of the book, supervising the complex printing process of the time from engraving to hand coloring of individual plates. In 1787 Redouté had the opportunity to visit England where he had gone to join his patron L'Hértier in London. There he met the Anglo-Italian engraver Francesco Bartolozzi, whose work was to have a profound effect on Redouté's technique. Bartolozzi had perfected a method of stipple engraving whereby minute dots rather than the usual incised lines predominated.

This new technique allowed for greater nuance of tone and shading and made color printing possible. The engraved metal plate was inked by hand with various colors carefully applied to the areas where they would appear on the finished print. Only one impression was possible for each inking and then the plate would have to be wiped clean and colored again for the next pull. The process was far more labor-intensive and costly than the more common practice of hand coloring black and white engravings with watercolors, but the results were much more effective.

When he returned to France the following year, Redouté began to gradually adopt Bartolozzi's methods for his own work. In the meantime L'Hértier had begun another project, the *Sertum Angelicum*, a book illustrating some of the many plants recently introduced in the gardens at Kew. This homage to English collecting appeared in 1789 with 22 plates by Redouté and 13 by James Sowerby, another of L'Hértier's protégés. About this time Redouté's work attracted the notice of a renowned Dutch flower painter who had been active in

Paris for many years, Gérard van Spaendonck. This artist was not only a fine painter, he was also socially and politically well connected.

Once again Redouté seemed to be leading a charmed life. In an age when talent alone did not guarantee success, Redouté was fortunate indeed to have friends who were both powerful and influential. Through the intercession of van Spaendonck, Redouté was invited to contribute his original drawings to the *Vélins du Rio*, a famous collection of natural-history drawings and paintings on vellum by the most noted artists of France that had been started in the proceeding century by Louis XIII's brother Gaston, Duc d'Orléans, and continued in each succeeding reign. Before he knew it, Redouté had received a royal appointment as official draftsman to the Queen, Marie-Antoinette, a post more honorary than onerous.

This official recognition would not benefit Redouté for long, since the old regime was soon to be swept away by the French Revolution. Whether protected by his art or his politics, Redouté not only survived the turmoil of the times, he actually prospered. His loyalties were quickly transferred to the Convention, and his status was duly upheld. In 1792 van Spaendonck was again instrumental in his friend's advancement when he arranged for Redouté to be appointed as draftsman to the Académies des Sciences. When that institution was dissolved the following year, both Redouté and his younger brother were placed as artists on the staff of the new Muséum d'Histoire Naturelle, as the former Jardin du Roi was now called.

Redouté continued to work on the *Vélins,* which had been transferred from the former royal library to the museum. Altogether he contributed more than 500 flower paintings to the series. At the same time he was at work on hundreds of engraved plates for several botanical books and journals in various stages of production. By the 1790's Redouté had developed his own distinctive style, based largely on the combined influence of L'Hértier and van Spaendonck. From the former he had acquired the scientific background needed to command respect in academic circles, and from the latter he had learned to render color and tone with subtlety and finesse.

Van Spaendonck, like Bartolozzi, was also proficient in the technique of color stipple engraving, and during this period Redouté mastered its use. In 1798 the artist turned his attention to a new publication devoted to succulent plants with a text by a young Swiss botanist, Augustin-Tyramus de Candolle, entitled *Plantarum Succulentarum Historia*, or *Plantes Grasses* in French. This work is notable for being the first entirely illustrated by Redouté himself, as well as the first to make use of his method of color printing from stipple-engraved plates. It is also the only book for which Redouté would ever do all of his own engraving. For the first time, with this work Redouté also broke away from a time-honored convention of botanical art by not placing a ruled line around the composition. Henceforth, Redouté would never again confine his drawings within a ruled framework.

The year 1798 was important in another way as a turning point in Redouté's life for this was the year that he entered into the service of Josephine Bonaparte. The extravagant wife of the First Consul Napoleon and future Empress of the French had just purchased, on credit, a large estate not far from Paris called Malmaison and had undertaken to restore it. No expense was to be spared, even though funds were not yet in hand, to renovate not only the château but also the extensive grounds. Josephine conceived of turning her gardens into something more than the usual pleasant retreat of pretty flowers and trimmed shrubbery. She envisioned a botanical Eden filled with the rare foreign plants that were then so much in vogue. A vast greenhouse was to be constructed, and a staff of expert botanists and gardeners was to be employed. A menagerie of wild and domestic animals was another feature that enhanced Josephine's own private realm, which combined the scientific with the picturesque.

Redouté was appointed to record and, in effect, to promote this enterprise. In time he became a true friend of the Empress Josephine and remained with her until her death in 1814. In return he received a generous salary and free time to devote to various publications. During the years that Redouté spent working at Malmaison, he accomplished much of his finest work.

In 1802 the first installment of what many consider to be Redouté's masterpiece appeared, *Les Liliacées*, with text by de Candolle. Perhaps as an indication of the artist's growing fame, his name alone appears on the title pages of the several parts rather than that of the botanical authority. The following year Ventenat's *Jardin de la Malmaison* began to come out, completed in 1805 in two volumes with 120 color plates by Redouté and documenting the developing collection of rare plants at Josephine's estate. A decade later, starting in 1812, *Description des plantes rares cultivées à Malmaison et à Navarre* by Aimé Bonpland began to appear with 52 out of the 64 color plates by Redouté. Together these three great publications have come to be regarded as Redouté's best. In them scientific accuracy and artistic excellence are combined to a degree that Redouté was never again to attain on quite such a high level. Stipple engraving is utilized to perfection throughout to interpret delicate drawings that are both beautiful and correct.

Les Liliacées is the largest and most ambitious work ever undertaken by Redouté, published by the artist himself in 80 installments between 1802 and 1816. Each part contains six plates excepting the last, which has 12, making up a total of 486 plates in eight folio volumes, illustrating 476 different species. An explanatory text accompanies each section with Latin botanical classifications and

French commentary contributed by one of Redouté's botanist collaborators, outlining each plant's habitat and history. Publication was limited to 200 copies, plus an additional 18 special copies with all the plates hand-finished by Redouté himself. (In the printing process employed, each color plate received enhancement by an artisan's brush dipped in watercolor.)

In spite of its title, *Les Liliacées* is devoted not only to plants of the lily family but also to representatives of other families of plants belonging to the group called "petaloid monocotyledons." Consequently, such plants as the iris and the amaryllis are included. The book has never been republished in its entirety. Because of the beauty of the illustrations, many copies have unfortunately been cut up by print sellers to provide framed pictures.

Although the Empress Josephine did not directly sponsor the undertaking herself, it could not have been possible without her support. Through her influence the Minister of the Interior, Chaptal, to whom Redouté diplomatically dedicated the work, ordered 80 sets. These copies were deposited in museums around the country or distributed by Talleyrand, the Foreign Minister, as Imperial gifts to important members of the European intellectual community to promote the reputation of the French art and science. Finally, Josephine purchased the original drawings on vellum from the artist even before the series was completed, and these descended as heirlooms in her family. A representative selection of choice plates from this compilation of prints and drawings is reproduced on the following pages.

His next major effort was *Les Roses*, begun at Malmaison in 1817 after the death of Josephine and continuing through 1824. This ultimately became Redouté's most famous work and the one that has been most often reproduced. The Empress had loved roses and amassed a collection numbering in the hundreds of species. Her rose gardens provided the inspiration for this work. Technically and artistically the equal of *Les Liliacées*, *Les Roses* had always been more popular with the general public than with the scientific community. Though just as botanically exact as before, Redouté's compositions now began to reflect greater artistic license. The roses became more important in themselves as the subjects of still-life arrangements, while the lilies had been more the subordinant subjects of documentation.

In his personal life Redouté continued to be a survivor. Long before the death of Josephine, following her divorce from Napoleon, he had been appointed drawing master to the new Empress Marie Louise. Despite his Napoleonic connections, with the Bourbon restoration starting in 1815 he was accepted first by Louis XVIII and then received the Legion of Honor from the next king, Charles X, in 1825. At the death of his old friend van Spaendonck in 1822, he was made drawing master at the natural history museum. He became a teacher of the Princesses Louise and Marie, both children of the Duc d'Orleans. After the accession to the throne of their father as King Louis-Philippe following the 1830 Revolution, this connection led to Redouté's last court position from the new Queen Marie-Amélie as *Peintre de fleurs du Cabinet*.

In his last years Redouté labored on, producing such important works as *Choix des plus belles fleurs*, published between 1827 and 1833 and containing 144 color plates, in addition to numerous others. In 1828 he was visited by Audubon in his studio. The great master of flowers met the great master of the birds, and the two exchanged examples of their work. Redouté even recommended Audubon to the ruling family. After the meeting Audubon commented on Redouté's love of natural subjects rendered in the animated manner when he wrote in his diary; "Old Redouté dislikes all that is not nature alone." Years before, Napoleon had asked the artist why he did not devote himself to themes grander and more heroic than floral models could provide. Quoting from the Roman emperor, Redouté replied that he agreed with Caesar that it was better to establish supremacy in a lowly field than risk failure in a more exalted area.

The discovery of previously unknown work by any artist is always an exciting event. The second group of 84 plates reproduced here record just such a find. These hand-tinted lithographs were recently found bound together without text or title page in an old library. All are signed in the plate by Redouté and inscribed by lithographers in his employ such as Pointel du Portail, F. Courtin, and A. Prevost. The publisher was Charles Boivin, Boulevard Poissoniere No. 23, for the largest portion, or Clement (Ainé) at No. 3 Quai Voltaire, Paris, for the remainder, indicating that these prints are probably part of not one but two different series. Neither set corresponds to any recorded work by Redouté.

In style all are very similar and resemble the late phase of the artist's work. Each plate depicts a small bouquet, hardly more than a nosegay, of two to three flowers arranged in a dainty spray. In handling they are neither overly delicate nor excessively bold, but seem to strike a happy balance. They may safely be dated circa 1835-1840 and may well have been published at the very end of Redouté's life or even posthumously. It is possible that they represent the publisher's proof of aborted editions and may prove to be unique. On June 20, 1840, Redouté died the day after he was stricken in his studio while working on his last flower painting. The picture is said to have portrayed a lily given to him by his daughter and sole companion in old age. In his lifetime of 80 years he had grown from an obscure wandering painter who was little more than a hack decorator to a widely recognized master of his genre, honored and admired for his skill throughout the world, whose remarkable work has never been surpassed.

Graham Arader, 1991

List of Plates*

BOUQUETS

Géranium et Jacinthe   1
Pois vivaces et ne m'oubliez pas   2
Dilenia et Oeillet panaché   3
Laurier blanc et Liserons   4
Anémone, Renoncules et Cinéraires   5
Clématite et Rose à cent feuilles   6
Pensées et Anémone vivace   7
Géranium, Rose jaune et fleurs de lin vivace   8
Oeillets, Cyclamén et Pensées   9
Camélia, Pois de senteur et Anémone   10
Oreilles d'Ours et Poirier du Japon   11
Géranium, Chrysanthème et Rose mousse   12
Dahlia et Pervenche   13
Rose Thé blanche et Benoite écarlate   14
Belle de jour et Altéa   15
Camélia blanc et Giroflée jaune   16
Dahlia et Capucines   17
Primevère de la Chine et Ellebore   18
Marguerites et Oeillet de la Chine   19
Coréopsis et Eglantier   20
Rose ponceau du Bengale et Pervenche   21
Chrysanthèmes   22
Oenotera et Zinnia   23

Narcisses blancs doubles et Camelia panaché   24
Giroflée rouge et Géranium blanc   25
Primevère et Narcisse double   26
Tigridia et Pavenia   27
Oeillets   28
Giroflée blanche et Chrysanthème   29
Laurier rose double et Philia   30
Mauve et Bignonia   31
Astromeria, Géranium et Pensée   32
Rose panachée et Chrysanthème   33
Chevre-Feuille et Oeillet d'Inde   34
Rose à cent feuille et Couleur de souffre   35
Coquelicot et Bleuet   36
Eglantiers, Oenotera et Lobélia   37
Iris et Gorteria   38
Azalea et Chrysanthème   39
Metrosideros, Anémone double   40
Gordonia, Campanule et Benoit jaune   41
Passiflore, Chrysanthème et Lin   42
Giroflée et Arctotis   43
Iris, Anémone et Géranium   44
Mauve et Ixia   45
Oeillet et Oranger Pompoleon   46
Pivoine, Renoncule et Géranium   47
Hemerocalle et Petunia   48

*Publisher's Note: *Plates are numbered as the originals. At the risk of some inconsistency we have preserved Redouté's spelling throughout.*

Accacia rose et Ibiscus   49
Sistus et Nigella   50
Hortensia, Cinéraire et Fuchsia   51
Volcameria, Lin vivace, Xeranthemum
    et Pensée   52
Rose noire et Seneçon lilas   53
Tulipe anglaise et Chrysanthème   54
Rhododendrum, Thunbergia et
    Volubilis   55
Lis blanc, Pois de senteur et
    Gallardia   56
Glauxinia et Géranium de Ste
    Hélène   57
Grenadier à fleurs blanches, petit
    Soleil   58
Lis orange, Nenuphar bleu   59
Oeillets et Eglantiers   60
Rose à cent feuilles et Cinéraires   61
Rose Thé et Pensées   62
Rose belle Véronique et Pois de
    senteur   63
Rose boule de neige et Phlox   64
Rose mousseuse et Calsa Palustrisa   65
Rose bengale à Coeur blanc et
    Hépathique   66

Rose rouge des 4 saisons et Coronille
    emerus   67
Rose Bengale des prés et Pensées   68
Rose bengale élégant et Oreilles
    d'Ours   69
Roses jaunes et Cinéraires   70
Rose a cent feuilles et Cyclaméne   71
Rose Triomphe du Luxemborg et
    Adonis   72
Rose d'amour et Souci de vigne   73
Rose Bengale superbe et Lupin   74
Rose quatre saisons rouge et
    Thumbergia alata   75
Rose et Anémone étoilée   76
Rose jaune et Phlox   77
Rose Marie Antoinette et Petunia   78
Rose Pompadour et Petunia   79
Rose, feuilles de Celeri et
    Gallardia   80
Rose Bengale strombio et Giroflée
    simple   81
Rose Cent feuilles simple et
    Gallardia   82
Rose hybide de Provins et
    Chrysanthème   83
Rose à cent feuilles et Capucines   84

LILIES

Iris Squalens (original watercolor)
Gordonia Lubescens   1
Lachenale Tricolore   2
Lachenalia Tricolor

Hemerocalle du Jappon   3
Hemerocallis Japponica
Iris Pâle   6
Iris Pallida

Lilium Pomponium   7
Glayeul de Merian   11
Gladiolos Merianus
Hemerocallis Coerulea   18
Anamenia Coriacea   22
Cannes a sucre réduites   23
Iris double Bulbe   29
Iris Lisyrinchium
Glayeul en Pointe   36
Gladiolus Cuspidatus
Iris Tubereuse   48
Iris Tuberosa
Morée à longue Gaine   56
Moroea Vaginata
Glayeul couleur de Chair   65
Gladiolus Carneus
Fritillaire de Perse   67
Fritillaria Persica
Pitcairnie faux-Ananas   75
Pitcairnia Bromeliaefolia
Strelitzia de la Reine   77
Strelitzia Reginae
Strelitzia de la Reine   78
Strelitzia Reginae
Ixia jaune et brun   86
Ixia fusco-citrina
Lis à fleur Pendante   105
Lilium Penduliflorum
Balisier Flasque   107
Canna Flaccida
Amaryllis Ondulée   115
Amaryllis Undulata
Ornithogale à longues bractées   120
Ornithogalum Longibracteatum
Glayeul en Gueule   123
Gladiolus Ringens
Ixia Tricolore   129

Ixia Tricolor
Fritillaria Imperialis   131
Lis des Pyrénées   145
Lilium Pyrenaicum
Heliconia des Perroquets   151
Heliconia Psitaccorum
Scille du Perou   167
Scilla Peruviana
Massonia Pustuleuse   183
Massonia Pustulata
Uvulaire Perfoliée   184
Uvularia Perfoliata
Iris de Perse   189
Iris Persica
Lis Blanc   199
Lilium Candidum
Balisier des Indes   201
Canna Indica
Iris faux-Xyphium   212
Iris Xyphioides
Asphodele Jaune   223
Asphodeles Luteus
Colchique Tacheté   238
Colchicum Variegatum
Ephémère Droite   239
Tradescantia Erecta
Iris Naine à fleurs violettes   261
Iris Pumilia floribus Violaceis
Amarillis à feuilles recourbées   274
Amaryllis Curvifolia
Tritoma à long épi   291
Tritoma Uvaria
Iris à Feuilles de Gramen   299
Iris Graminea
Iris de Swert   306
Iris Swertu

Bananier à fleurs écarlates 308
Musa Coccinea
Iris Brune 318
Iris Lurida
Balisier Géant 331
Canna Gigantea
Ixia Safrané 335
Ixia Crocata
Iris à couleurs changeantes 339
Iris Versicolor
Sowerbée Junciforme 341
Sowerbea Juncea
Crinum d'Asie 348
Crinum Asiaticum
Iris Batarde 349
Iris Spuria
Iris Fétide 351
Iris Foetidissima
Pancrace à liges penchées 358
Pancratium declinatum
Commeline douteuse 359
Commelina dubia
Lis nain 378
Lilium pumilum
Cyrtanthe oblique 381
Cyrtanthus obliquus
Heliconia à petite tige 382
Heliconia humilis
Heliconia à petite tige 383
Heliconia humilis
Cyrtanthe à feuilles étroites 388
Cyrtanthus angustifolius

Ail à tête ronde 391
Allium sphaerocephalon
Ananas sauvage 396
Bromeliae pinguin
Glayeul à fleurs droites 399
Gladiolus Strictifloras
Neottie à fleurs roses 404
Neottia speciosa
Pancrace à belles fleurs 412
Pancratium Speciosum
Vératre noir 416
Veratrum nigrum
Ixia à fleurs de phlox 432
Ixia phlogiflora
Ornithogale doré 439
Ornithogalum aureum
Veltheimia glauque 440
Veltheimiaglauca
Tulipe à fleurs pointues 445
Tulipa Cornuta
Amaryllis peu élevée 450
Amaryllis humilis
Iris double bulbe, à fleur violet-pale 458
Iris sisyrinchium. Var.
Lilium Tigrinum 475
Iris à trois fleurs 481
Iris Triflora
Iris de Luze 483
Iris Luziana
Ferrarie ferrariole 484
Ferraria ferrariola

Bouquets

Géranium et Jacinthe

P.J. Redouté. — 1

Pois vivaces et ne m'oubliez pas

P.J. Redouté. — 2

Dilenia et Oeillet panaché

P.J. Redouté. — 3

Laurier blanc et Liserons

P.J. Redouté. — 4

Anémone, Renoncules et Cinéraires

P.J. Redouté. — 5

Clématite et Rose à cent feuilles

P.J. Redouté. — 6

Pensées et Anémone vivace

P.J. Redouté. — 7

Géranium, Rose jaune et fleurs de lin vivace

P.J. Redouté. — 8

Oeillets, Cyclamén et Pensées

P.J. Redouté. — 9

Camélia, Pois de senteur et Anémone

P.J. Redouté. — 10

Oreilles d'Ours et Poirier du Japon

P.J. Redouté. — 11

Géranium, Chrysanthème et Rose mousse

P.J. Redouté. — 12

Dahlia et Pervenche

P.J. Redouté. — 13

Rose Thé blanche et Benoite écarlate

P.J. Redouté. — 14

Belle de jour et Altéa

P.J. Redouté. — 15

Camélia blanc et Giroflée jaune

P.J. Redouté. — 16

Dahlia et Capucines

P.J. Redouté. — 17

Primevère de la Chine et Ellebore

P.J. Redouté. — 18

Marguerites et Oeillet de la Chine

P.J. Redouté. — 19

Coréopsis et Églantier

P.J. Redouté. — 20

Rose ponceau du Bengale et Pervenche

P.J. Redouté. — 21

Chrysanthèmes

P.J. Redouté. — 22

Oenotera et Zinnia

P.J. Redouté. — 23

Narcisses blancs doubles et Camelia panaché

P.J. Redouté. — 24

Giroflée rouge et Géranium blanc

P.J. Redouté. — 25

Primevère et Narcisse double

P.J. Redouté. — 26

Tigridia et Pavenia

P.J. Redouté. — 27

Oeillets

P.J. Redouté. — 28

Giroflée blanche et Chrysanthème

P.J. Redouté. — 29

Laurier rose double et Philia

Mauve et Bignonia

P.J. Redouté. — 31

Astromeria, Géranium et Pensée

P.J. Redouté. — 32

Rose panachée et Chrysanthème

P.J. Redouté. — 33

Chevre-Feuille et Oeillet d'Inde

P.J. Redouté. — 34

Rose à cent feuille et Couleur de souffre

P.J. Redouté. — 35

Coquelicot et Bleuet

P.J. Redouté. — 36

Eglantiers, Oenotera et Lobélia

P.J. Redouté. — 37

Iris et Gorteria

P.J. Redouté. — 38

Azalea et Chrysanthème

P.J. Redouté. — 39

Metrosideros, Anémone double

P.J. Redouté. — 40

Gordonia, Campanule et Benoit jaune

P.J. Redouté. — 41

Passiflore, Chrysanthème et Lin

P.J. Redouté. — 42

Giroflée et Arctotis

P.J. Redouté. — 43

Iris, Anémone et Géranium

P.J. Redouté. — 44

Mauve et Ixia

P.J. Redouté. — 45

Oeillet et Oranger Pompoleon

P.J. Redouté. — 46

Pivoine, Renoncule et Géranium

P.J. Redouté. — 47

Hemerocalle et Petunia

P.J. Redouté. — 48

Accacia rose et Ibiscus

P.J. Redouté. — 49

Sistus et Nigella

P.J. Redouté. — 50

Hortensia, Cinéraire et Fuchsia

P.J. Redouté. — 51

Volcameria, Lin vivace, Xeranthemum et Pensée

Rose noire et Seneçon lilas

P.J. Redouté. — 53

Tulipe anglaise et Chrysanthème

P.J. Redouté. — 54

Rhododendrum, Thunbergia et Volubilis

P.J. Redouté. — 55

Lis blanc, Pois de senteur et Gallardia

P.J. Redouté. — 56

Glauxinia et Géranium de Ste Hélène

Grenadier à fleurs blanches, petit Soleil

P.J. Redouté. — 58

Lis orange, Nenuphar bleu

P.J. Redouté. — 59

Oeillets et Eglantiers

P.J. Redouté. — 60

Rose à cent feuilles et Cinéraires

P.J. Redouté. — 61

Rose Thé et Pensées

P.J. Redouté. — 62

Rose belle Véronique et Pois de senteur

Rose boule de neige et Phlox

P.J. Redouté. — 64

Rose mousseuse et Calsa Palustrisa

Rose bengale à Coeur blanc et Hépathique

P.J. Redouté. — 66

Rose rouge des 4 saisons et Coronille emerus

P.J. Redouté. — 67

Rose Bengale des prés et Pensées

P.J. Redouté. — 68

Rose bengale élégant et Oreilles d'Ours

P.J. Redouté. — 69

Roses jaunes et Cinéraires

P.J. Redouté. — 70

Rose a cent feuilles et Cyclaméne

P.J. Redouté. — 71

Rose Triomphe du Luxemborg et Adonis

P.J. Redouté. — 72

Rose d'amour et Souci de vigne

P.J. Redouté. — 73

Rose Bengale superbe et Lupin

P.J. Redouté. — 74

Rose quatre saisons rouge et Thumbergia alata

P.J. Redouté. — 75

Rose et Anémone étoilée

P.J. Redouté. — 76

Rose jaune et Phlox

P.J. Redouté. — 77

Rose Marie Antoinette et Petunia

P.J. Redouté. — 78

Rose Pompadour et Petunia

P.J. Redouté. — 79

Rose, feuilles de Celeri et Gallardia

P.J. Redouté. — 80

Rose Bengale strombio et Giroflée simple

P.J. Redouté. — 81

Rose Cent feuilles simple et Gallardia

P.J. Redouté. — 82

Rose hybide de Provins et Chrysanthème

P.J. Redouté. — 83

Rose à cent feuilles et Capucines

P.J. Redouté. — 84

Lilies

Iris Squalens

P.J. Redouté.

Gordonia Lubescens

P.J. Redouté. — 1

Lachenalia Tricolor   *Lachenale Tricolore*

P.J. Redouté. — 2

Hemerocallis Japponica   *Hemerocalle du Jappon*

P.J. Redouté. — 3

Iris Pallida   Iris Pâle

P.J. Redouté. — 6

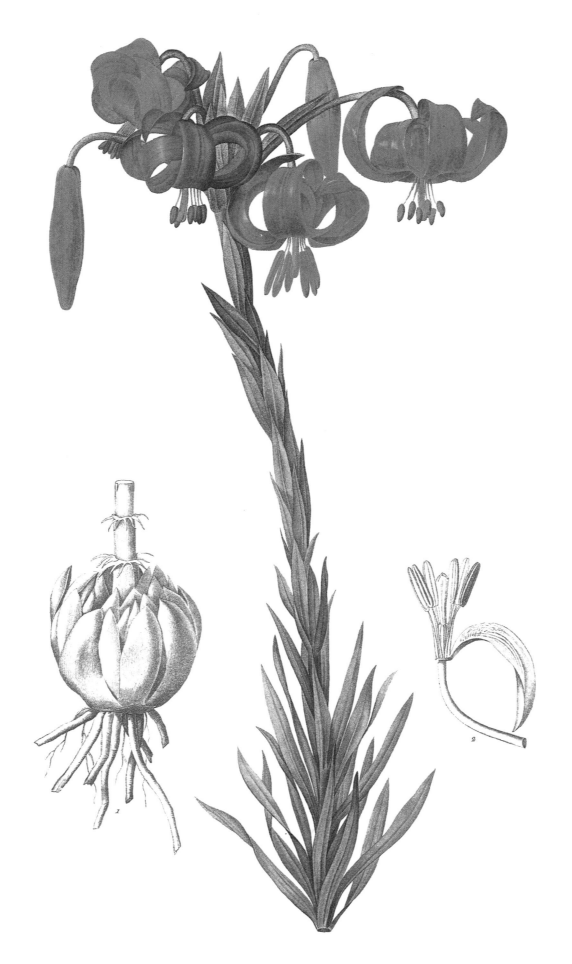

Lilium Pomponium

P.J. Redouté. — 7

Gladiolos Merianus   *Glayeul de Merian*

P.J. Redouté. — 11

Hemerocallis Coerulea

P.J. Redouté. — 18

Anamenia Coriacea

P.J. Redouté. — 22

Cannes a sucre réduites

P.J. Redouté. — 23

Iris Lisyrinchium   *Iris double Bulbe*

P.J. Redouté. — 29

Gladiolus Cuspidatus   *Glayeul en Pointe*

P.J. Redouté. — 36

Iris Tuberosa   *Iris Tubereuse*

P.J. Redouté. — 48

Moroea Vaginata   *Morée à longue Gaine*

P.J. Redouté. — 56

Gladiolus Carneus　　*Glayeul couleur de Chair*

Fritillaria Persica　　　*Fritillaire de Perse*

P.J. Redouté. — 67

Pitcairnia Bromeliaefolia   *Pitcairnie faux-Ananas*

P.J. Redouté. — 75

Strelitzia Reginae   *Strelitzia de la Reine*

Strelitzia Reginae   *Strelitzia de la Reine*

P.J. Redouté. — 78

Ixia fusco-citrina   *Ixia jaune et brun*

P.J. Redouté. — 86

Lilium Penduliflorum   *Lis à fleur Pendante*

P.J. Redouté. — 105

Canna Flaccida   *Balisier Flasque*

P.J. Redouté. — 107

Amaryllis Undulata   *Amaryllis Ondulée*

P.J. Redouté. — 115

Ornithogalum Longibracteatum   *Ornithogale à longues bractées*

P.J. Redouté. — 120

Gladiolus Ringens   *Glayeul en Gueule*

P.J. Redouté. — 123

Ixia Tricolor   *Ixia Tricolore*

P.J. Redouté. — 129

Fritillaria Imperialis

P.J. Redouté. — 131

Lilium Pyrenaicum   *Lis des Pyrénées*

P.J. Redouté. — 145

Heliconia Psitaccorum   *Heliconia des Perroquets*

P.J. Redouté. — 151

Scilla Peruviana   *Scille du Perou*

P.J. Redouté. — 167

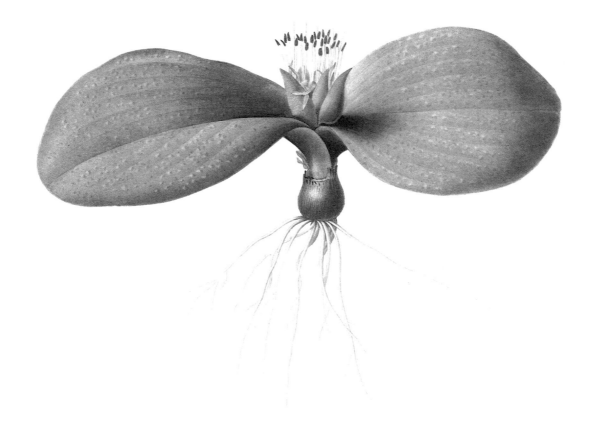

Massonia Pustulata   *Massonia Pustuleuse*

P.J. Redouté. — 183

Uvularia Perfoliata   *Uvulaire Perfoliée*

P.J. Redouté. — 184

Iris Persica   *Iris de Perse*

P.J. Redouté. — 189

Lilium Candidum   *Lis Blanc*

P.J. Redouté. — 199

Canna Indica   *Balisier des Indes*

P.J. Redouté. — 201

Iris Xyphioides   *Iris faux-Xyphium*

P.J. Redouté. — 212

Asphodeles Luteus   *Asphodele Jaune*

P.J. Redouté. — 223

Colchicum Variegatum   *Colchique Tacheté*

P.J. Redouté. — 238

Tradescantia Erecta　　　*Ephémère Droite*

P.J. Redouté. — 239

Iris Pumilia floribus Violaceis   *Iris Naine à fleurs violettes*

Amaryllis Curvifolia   *Amarillis à feuilles recourbées*

P.J. Redouté. — 274

Tritoma Uvaria   *Tritoma à long épi*

P.J. Redouté. — 291

Iris Graminea   *Iris à Feuilles de Gramen*

P.J. Redouté. — 299

Iris Swertu   *Iris de Swert*

P.J. Redouté. — 306

Musa Coccinea   *Bananier à fleurs écarlates*

P.J. Redouté. — 308

Iris Lurida   Iris Brune

P.J. Redouté. — 318

Canna Gigantea   *Balisier Géant*

P.J. Redouté. — 331

Ixia Crocata   *Ixia Safrané*

P.J. Redouté. — 335

Iris Versicolor   *Iris à couleurs changeantes*

P.J. Redouté. — 339

Sowerbea Juncea　　　*Sowerbée Junciforme*

P.J. Redouté. — 341

Crinum Asiaticum   *Crinum d'Asie*

P.J. Redouté. — 348

Iris Spuria   *Iris Batarde*

P.J. Redouté. — 349

Iris Foetidissima   *Iris Fétide*

P.J. Redouté. — 351

Pancratium declinatum   *Pancrace à liges penchées*

P.J. Redouté. — 358

Commelina dubia   *Commeline douteuse*

P.J. Redouté. — 359

Lilium pumilum   *Lis nain*

P.J. Redouté. — 378

Cyrtanthus obliquus   *Cyrtanthe oblique*

P.J. Redouté. — 381

Heliconia humilis   *Heliconia à petite tige*

Heliconia humilis   *Heliconia à petite tige*

P.J. Redouté. — 383

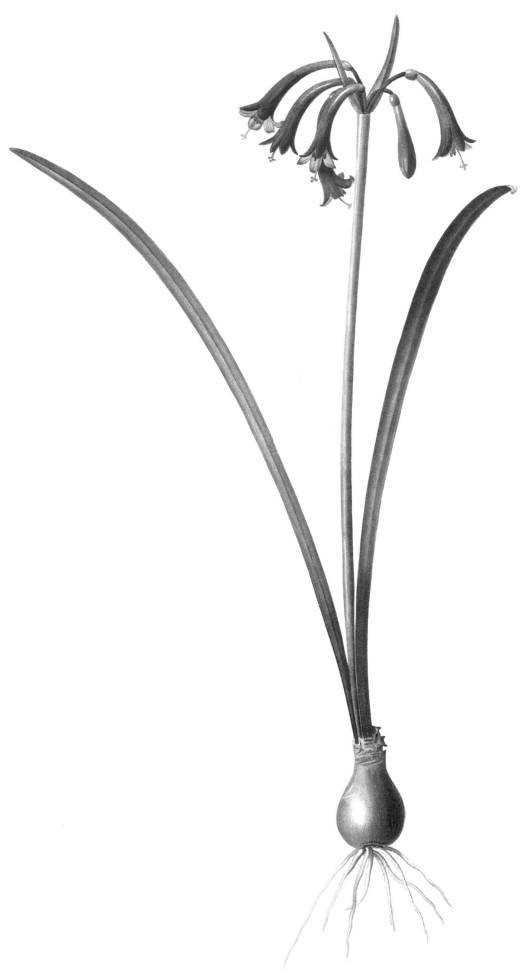

Cyrtanthus angustifolius   *Cyrtanthe à feuilles étroites*

P.J. Redouté. — 388

Allium sphaerocephalon   *Ail à tête ronde*

P.J. Redouté. — 391

Bromeliae pinguin   *Ananas sauvage*

P.J. Redouté. — 396

Gladiolus Strictifloras   *Glayeul à fleurs droites*

P.J. Redouté. — 399

Neottia speciosa   *Neottie à fleurs roses*

P.J. Redouté. — 404

Pancratium Speciosum   *Pancrace à belles fleurs*

P.J. Redouté. — 412

Veratrum nigrum   *Vératre noir*

P.J. Redouté. — 416

Ixia phlogiflora   *Ixia à fleurs de phlox*

P.J. Redouté. — 432

Ornithogalum aureum   *Ornithogale doré*

P.J. Redouté. — 439

Veltheimiaglauca   *Veltheimia glauque*

P.J. Redouté. — 440

Tulipa Cornuta   *Tulipe à fleurs pointues*

P.J. Redouté. — 445

Amaryllis humilis   *Amaryllis peu élevée*

P.J. Redouté. — 450

Iris sisyrinchium. Var.   *Iris double bulbe, à fleur violet-pale*

Lilium Tigrinum

Iris Triflora   *Iris à trois fleurs*

P.J. Redouté. — 481

Iris Luziana   *Iris de Luze*

P.J. Redouté. — 483

Ferraria ferrariola   *Ferrarie ferrariole*

P.J. Redouté. — 484